WELCOME TO

KESWICK

ON DERWENTWATER

SMALL TOWN WINNER
BRITAIN IN BLOOM

David Quainton

Travellers approaching Keswick from the West on the morning of Friday 20 November 2009 were met by this view of the road which had become a river overnight. The channel of the River Greta is on the far side of the field on the right.

Gill Bulch

This photograph, blurred due to the long exposure necessary in the low light conditions, illustrates extremely well the full force of the Greta and the astonishing speed of the current at 8.00 pm on Thursday 19 November. The Youth Hostel walkway on the left is just under water.

This view, also from Station Road Bridge, shows the Greta in full flow towards the Memorial Footbridge at about 8.00 pm on Thursday 19 November 2009.

This old mill, dating back to the 1790's, opposite Lower Fitz Park on the Greta was converted twentyfour years ago into flats and workshops. The flood caused damage to the lower right corner of the building, which later caused the wall to collapse, see above.

Keswick Mountain Rescue team were heavily involved with rescuing residents from the floods. Here they are seen with their inflatable rescue boat at High Hill near the service station.

About 1.30 pm on Thursday the river overtopped the retaining wall and flooded the road on both sides of the nearby Greta Bridge, which was later closed for safety reasons. **Inset:** before the overtopping of the dyke a thumb or two might have been of help to stem the flow!

Gill Bulch

Greta Bridge as the water almost completely fills the arches at 1.10 pm on the Thursday. The bridge was closed soon after this picture was taken, as the enormous force of the water trying to get under the bridge could have caused it to collapse without warning.

Helen Foot

A view of the upstream side of Greta Bridge at about 2.00 pm. This photograph vividly illustrates the immense force of the water pushing against the stonework of the bridge. The arches are almost filled with the flow and water is forced up onto the central buttress.

WELCOME TO FITZ PARK

LAWN TENNIS, PUTTING,
BOWLING GREEN

ORNAMENTAL GARDENS,
RIVERSIDE WALK, SENSORY GARDEN

A KESWICK ARBORETUM SITE

DOGS WELCOME ON A LEAD - NO CYCLING

Gill Bulch

Fitz Park early in the afternoon of Thursday 19 November. The river has already broken through onto the Penrith Road on the right.

The Penrith road about 1.30 pm on Thursday. the river has crossed the road to flood the houses opposite.

Keswick Reminder

Looking back towards the town centre from the flooded Penrith road.

Tarmac in Fitz Park, ripped up by the floodwater.

Keswick Rugby Union Ground, flooded once more!

The power of the river in flood.

A bleak view over the flooded Rugby Pitch.

Keswick Mountain Rescue team rescuing residents from their flooded homes by boat at High Hill.

A rescuer braves the flood in Crosthwaite Road.

Flooded Keswick Football Club building opened on 24/10/09.

13

Residents of the Wesleyan Chapel Flats near Booths Supermarket were evacuated by the fire brigade on Thursday 19 November at about 1300 hours in pouring rain.

Keswick Reminder

David Quainton

This photograph was taken just across the road from the flats, almost 18 hours later, at Booths Supermarket. The photographer had made his way into Keswick on foot from Portinscale, wearing his waders. **Inset**: The supermarket car and trolley park flooded out.

Jackie Wilkinson

Derwentwater overflowed onto the Borrowdale Road in several places, making it impassable. This photograph, taken on Friday 20 November from a point about half way between the Ashness Bridge junction and Kettlewell car park, shows the Borrowdale road and Derwentwater as one, with Catbells in the background.

The road approaching Ouse Bridge from Castle Inn on Thursday 19 November 2009. Note the roof of the submerged car in the centre of the picture and the tractor on the far left. Caravans in the caravan park at Ousebridge were also flooded. See next page.

Flooded caravans on the Ousebridge caravan park photographed on Friday 20 November 2009 from the road between Armathwaite Hall Hotel and Ousebridge.

Jackie Wilkinson

At the time of writing Ousebridge, along with many other bridges in the area, was still closed for safety reasons. Here the foundations of the bridge at the north east corner have been eroded by the force of the floodwater and the full damage has still to be assessed.

David Quainton

The field used for the annual Keswick Show had become a raging river, still very fast flowing, early on the morning of Friday 20 November. 2009. Hopefully it will be fully recovered for the next show on August Bank Holiday Monday, 2010.

Andy Byers

The Flooding and Destruction in and around Workington

Peter Cowman

The hamlet of Barepot on the north side of the Derwent suffered badly in the flooding as can be seen in this picture taken at 11.00 am on Friday 20 November 2009. Most of the town escaped the flooding but everybody suffered from the subsequent disruption to transport as a result of the unprecedented damage to all of the road and footbridges connecting the northside of Workington with the town centre.

Peter Cowman

Peter Cowman

Crossings Cottage, originally built for the level crossing keeper on the Cockermouth - Workington railway at Barepot, was badly affected in the floods. In this view, taken on the Sunday after the river burst it's banks, the river is still flowing along the front wall of the house. The inset picture was taken five days later on the 27 November 2009 when the river level had dropped by several feet.

William Peak

Upstream from Barepot is Camerton and Camerton Church. The road here shows Camerton Bridge which once crossed the Cockermouth to Workington Railway line, closed in 1963, but the bridge is still used to access Camerton Church. During the flood the river took a short cut along the line of the old railway and demolished the bridge. Pictures on the next page show that demolition by water taking place.

William Peak

20 November 2009 at 0830, part of the archway is still intact.

William Peak

20 November 2009 at 0835 and the archway has collapsed.

Pauline Scott

Later in the day the central pillar has collapsed.

Malcolm Minshaw

One week later and the river has returned to it's original channel.

Pauline Scott

Pauline Scott

There was extensive flooding on farmland near Camerton. and sheep were moved to safety on the Thursday evening but the cattle had to be left overnight and were able to find higher ground. The picture is looking towards Workington.
The cattle were brought back to the farm on the Friday for safety (see inset above).

Looking across to what is know as 'The Park' and Camerton. The original course of the river ran between the strip of land, upper left (line of old railway), and the trees on the far side(A). The river has now cut a new course, top right (B), effectively cutting the corner. Eight weeks after the flood most of the river water was still following the new channel. See the inset picture taken on 10 January 2010.

St Peter's Church at Camerton is on a U shaped peninsula of land surrounded by the river Derwent that was overtopped by the floodwaters, thus causing a lot of destruction in the churchyard.

Malcolm Minshaw

POLITE NOTICE

WHILST I ACCEPT THAT THE CURRENT STATE OF THE CHURCHYARD IS NOT VERY PLEASANT AND OBVIOUSLY DISTRESSING TO PEOPLE I ASK THAT VISITORS DO NOT TOUCH ANYTHING OR RE-POSITION ANY OF THE FALLEN OR DAMAGED HEADSTONES AS THE CHURCH AND CHURCHYARD ARE SUBJECT TO AN INSURANCE INSPECTION.
THANK YOU FOR YOUR PATIENCE.

Rev. Ian Grainger
Vicar
Tel: 01900 602162

Malcolm Minshaw

Such was the force of the current that many of the gravestones and memorials were toppled, broken or carried along by the floodwater, leaving a scene of destruction that will be difficult to put right.

Andy Byers

Peter Cowman

FOOTPATH CLOSED

Police HQ

Locally known as 'The Soapery' but officially called Hall Park View, this row of houses was inundated as the swollen river swept across Hall Park. The inset photograph taken on 21 December 2009 shows the cleanup still continuing one month after the floods.

Andy Byers

This picture taken just below The Yearl, on 23 November 2009, four days after the initial flooding, illustrates very well the destructive ability of the river when in full flood. Crossing Cottage, Barepot, can be seen in the background. Yearl is the local name for the weir.

Peter Cowman

Mill Field seen on the 20 November when the river was still in spate. The old mill and cottages can be seen in the distance.

Peter Cowman

Two days later on Sunday 22 November the water level has dropped, but water is still flowing along the old mill race and the river is still very full.

David Ramshaw

The most obvious evidence of the terrible power of the river in flood was the complete destruction of the main road bridge connecting north to south Workington which caused the tragic death of PC Bill Barker.
Traffic Officer PC Barker, 44, was directing motorists off the bridge in Workington "saving lives" when it suddenly collapsed and he was swept into the river.

PC Bill Barker receiving a long service and good conduct medal after 22 years service.

Workington's Christmas Tree with peoples' decorations to honour PC Bill Barker.

David Ramshaw

Cumbria Chief Constable Craig Mackey in a tribute to PC Bill Barker said: " *Bill was a wonderful police officer and a real family man. He leaves behind a wife and four children in their home in Egremont - two boys and two girls - aged between 8 and 16. He was due to celebrate his 45th birthday tomorrow. Bill is a hero who died saving the lives of others and our thoughts are with his family at this devastating time. He was a much loved friend, colleague and an inspiration to everyone he knew. - He will be sadly missed.*"

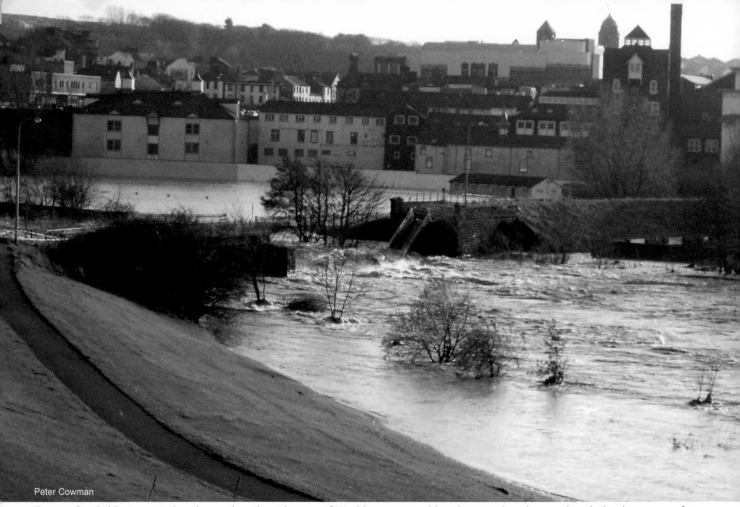

Peter Cowman

Every other bridge connecting the north and south parts of Workington was either destroyed or damaged such that it was unsafe to use. Here the Navvies footbridge, now also a cycle route, was completely destroyed. Photographed on Friday 20 November at 1500 hours.

Four views of Navvies Bridge after the flood. The destruction is such that it will take many months and maybe years before normal transport communications between the north and south of the town can be restored.

William Pea[...]

Here the harbour rail bridge was badly damaged by the floodwater.
The central concrete support has been undermined and washed out. Photographed on Friday 20 November with the river still in spate.

The bridge foundations have been disrupted and the movement has buckled the rails. The inset picture also shows that the Merchant's Quay tongue (in front of the bridge) has been washed away.

Peter Cowman

There are only two road bridges linking the north and south parts of Workington.
Calva Bridge was the only remaining road crossing after the collapse of North Bridge, but the central pier was undermined making it unusable.

David Ramshaw

David Ramshaw

Peter Cowman

WORKINGTON BRIDGE
BUILT A.D. 1841
THOMAS MILTON CIVIL ENGINEER
THOMAS NELSON BUILDER

Peter Cowman

The damage to the foundations of the central pillar and the partial collapse of the arch can clearly be seen in these images.
For 168 years Calva Bridge has survived the excesses of the River Derwent until the floods of 2009. See the datestone above.

41

Andy Byers

The Beginning of the Recovery

The only bridge that survived the floods undamaged carried the railway line between Workington and Maryport. This photograph shows emergency services and engineers checking the bridge at the height of the flood on Friday 20 November 2009.

The existing Carlisle to Barrow service stopped north of the river at Flimby which saw an immediate surge in passenger numbers after the floods. To make full use of the rail link Network Rail, on the 24 November, commenced the building of a temporary station north of the river opposite

Peter Cowman

Dunmail Park shopping centre, to be called 'Workington North'. Network Rail staff worked round the clock so that the station was opened only six days later. The station consists of two platforms linked by a footbridge, a waiting room, and a gravel car park. The platform was later extended to take longer trains. As well as the regular hourly service between Carlisle and Barrow extra shuttle trains were introduced at busy periods. This helped to get people to work and children to school. However, the lack of a road bridge meant that road vehicles had to travel over 20 miles via Cockermouth just to cross from one side of Workington to the other.

Peter Cowman

On 27 December the building of a temporary footbridge 300m upstream (east) of the Calva Bridge was undertaken by 3 Armoured Engineer Squadron, part of 22 Engineer Regiment, based in Tidworth. Over 200 soldiers were involved in the operation working day and night. **Above:** the army get to work on the earth foundations of the bridge on Hall Park.

Andy Byers

Foundations for the bridge and a road up to it, with a turning circle for buses were put in before assembling the bridge, hoisting and pushing it across the river. The construction effort ran to schedule with the nose landing on the far bank on Friday afternoon, and street furniture being installed over the weekend. From start to finish the bridge took one week to build.

Senior engineer Major Grant Kerr described how the crossing was made: The bridge was assembled on the south bank of the River Derwent and was pushed across the water, guided at the front by 12 lightweight truss sections acting as a "nose". The nose landed and then the bridge was pushed forwards. The bridge was then jacked down onto its bearings and the deck panels put in place.

Peter Cowman

BARKER CROSSING

BUILT BY 3 ARMD ENGR SQN DEC 2009

David Ramshaw

The finished bridge with a bus terminus at each side to provide transport between Workington Town Centre and the suburbs to the north. Schoolchildren could once more get to and from school and people could park their cars north of the river, catch the bus, cross the bridge, and catch another bus into the town centre for work or to shop. The bridge was named "Barker Crossing" in remembrance of PC Bill Barker.

David Ramshaw

The Tesco supermarket in Whitehaven is situated on the south side of the river next to the collapsed Northside bridge. Customers from the towns and villages north of the river had a 20 mile journey via Cockermouth to reach the store. To overcome this problem Tesco built a temporary "pop-up" 13,300 sq. ft. store on the north side of the river in just 13 days. The building was erected in just 24 hours.